Contents

Where is England?

England is a country in Europe which, together with Scotland and Wales, forms Great Britain. England is about three times the size of the Netherlands. Its capital city is London.

ENGLAND

London
★

Countries

England

by Christine Juarez

raintree

Raintree is an imprint of Capstone Global Library Limited, a company incorporated in England and Wales having its registered office at 264 Banbury Road, Oxford, OX2 7DY – Registered company number: 6695582

www.raintree.co.uk
myorders@raintree.co.uk

Edited by Erika L. Shores
Designed by Bobbie Nuytten
Picture research by Tracy Cummins
Production by Laura Manthe

ISBN 978 1 4747 1979 7 (hardback)
20 19 18 17 16
10 9 8 7 6 5 4 3 2 1

ISBN 978 1 4747 1986 5 (paperback)
21 20 19 18 17
10 9 8 7 6 5 4 3 2 1

British Library Cataloguing in Publication Data
A full catalogue record for this book is available from the British Library.

Photo Credits
Dreamstime: Peterguess, 22; Getty Images: Monty Rakusen, 17; iStockphotos: zoranm, 21; Newscom: LUKE MACGREGOR, 15; Shutterstock: anshar, 1, Bikeworldtravel, 11, CBCK, 5, Chrislofotos, 7, ekler, 4, Elena Shashkina, 13, Jonathan Feinstein, 19, Kaetana, cover, 1 (design element), Natalia Barsukova, 22, Ohmega1982, back cover (globe), Reddogs, 9, S.Borisov, cover

We would like to thank Gail Saunders-Smith, Ph.D., for her invaluable help in the preparation of this book.

Every effort has been made to contact copyright holders of material reproduced in this book. Any omissions will be rectified in subsequent printings if notice is given to the publisher.

All the internet addresses (URLs) given in this book were valid at the time of going to press. However, due to the dynamic nature of the internet, some addresses may have changed, or sites may have changed or ceased to exist since publication. While the author and publisher regret any inconvenience this may cause readers, no responsibility for any such changes can be accepted by either the author or the publisher.

Note to Parents and Teachers

The Countries series supports learning related to people, places and culture. This book describes and illustrates England. The images support early readers in understanding the text. The repetition of words and phrases helps early readers learn new words. This book also introduces early readers to subject-specific vocabulary, which is defined in the Glossary section. Early readers may need assistance to read some words and to use the Contents, Glossary, Read more, Websites and Index sections of the book.

Landforms

England has rolling hills, lakes and rivers. The Pennines are hills that run from central to northern England. The rainy Lake District is in the North West. The Thames is England's longest river.

Animals

Foxes, hares and mice are common
in England. About 230 kinds
of birds make England their home.
Another 200 kinds of birds pass
through England as they migrate.

Language and population

England is home to about 63 million people. Cities are crowded.

In cities, many people live in blocks of flats or terraced houses.

Most people speak English.

11

Food

A famous English dish is shepherd's pie. It is made of lamb mince and potato. England is also well known for fish and chips.

Celebrations

5 November is Guy Fawkes Night.
Guy Fawkes led a failed plot to blow
up the Houses of Parliament in 1605.
Every year, people celebrate the
plot with bonfires and fireworks.

Where people work

Most English people have service jobs. These jobs include teaching, banking and selling. Tourism has many service jobs. Tourists visit museums, churches and historical sites.

Transportation

Trains carry people to and from train stations across England. London's underground railway system is often called the Tube.

19

District
East

Famous sight

Buckingham Palace is in London.
The ruling king or queen lives
here when they are in London.
The palace holds royal events
and ceremonies.

Country facts

Name: England

Capital: London

Population: 63,000,000 (2015 estimate)

Size: 130,282 square kilometres (50,302 square miles)

Language: English

Main crops: wheat, barley, corn, rye, oats

Great Britain's flag

Money: pound

Glossary

capital city in a country where the government is based

celebrate do something fun on a special day

ceremony special actions, words or music performed to mark an important event

hare animal that looks like a large rabbit with long, strong back legs

island piece of land that is surrounded by water

landform natural feature of the land

language words used in a particular country or by a particular group of people

migrate move from one place to another in search of food

Parliament group that governs the United Kingdom

royal to do with a king or a queen

tourism business of taking care of visitors when they travel to a different country or place

Read more

London (The History Detective Investigates), Claudia Martin (Wayland, 2016)

England: A Benjamin Blog and His Inquisitive Dog Guide (Country Guides) Anita Ganeri (Raintree, 2015)

Websites

ngkids.co.uk/places/Ten-Horrible-Facts-About-London
Discover some fascinating facts about London.

www.royal.gov.uk/theroyalresidences/buckinghampalace/
buckinghampalace.aspx
All the information you ever wanted to know about Buckingham Palace!

Index